W9-CEP-553

Instant Nonfiction Writing Frames

by Rhonda Graff

NEW YORK · TORONTO · LONDON · AUCKLAND · SYDNEY
MEXICO CITY · NEW DELHI · HONG KONG · BUENOS AIRES

Teaching *Resources*

To my mother and father & Craig and Daniel with love

A special thank you to Liza Charlesworth, Gina Shaw,
and Jason Robinson for all their guidance and support

—R.G.

Cover and design by Jason Robinson

ISBN: 978-0-545-22416-1
Copyright © 2011 by Rhonda Graff

All rights reserved. Published by Scholastic Inc.
Printed in the U.S.A.

2 3 4 5 6 7 8 9 10   40   16 15 14 13 12 11

Contents

Introduction

Welcome to *Instant Nonfiction Writing Frames*! This book is designed to help students organize and plan a research paper or a nonfiction report. There are six topics presented, plus an Appendix. The Appendix is a valuable tool to use when planning these assignments because it allows you to customize and differentiate the assignments based on your needs and your students' abilities.

All reproducibles in this book are presented as frames for the children to fill in. These frames serve as guides to help children stay focused and organize their thoughts while gathering information and writing about a nonfiction topic. The frames provide structure, but allow the children to complete their writing in their own words. Each section has an icon. The icons are presented to visually assist students regarding what to write about in each section. Be sure to review the Appendix to choose supplemental handouts for each report based on students' needs and interests.

How to Use This Book

To start, peruse this resource and choose one of the presented topics. Then decide which pages need to be included in each child's report. Some students can complete the entire booklet, and you may want to include an illustration page, a glossary page, and a bibliography page from the Appendix. For another student, you may only want to include a beginning page from the booklet together with an illustration page and a bibliography page from the Appendix. You can customize what you feel is best for the given assignment and the given student. The Teacher Pages provide more specific information about the reproducibles throughout the book.

Helpful Hints

It will be helpful to model one section at a time so children will understand how to gather and write information about their given topics. Be sure to go step by step so they understand what is expected and how they can personalize their work. Be sure to model note-taking for the children so they understand how to gather information. Introduce the use of key words so the children don't copy word for word from a resource. Some students may use the frames as a place to gather notes and information as a pre-writing activity, if needed.

Children enjoy learning about nonfiction topics. This book will help them write about varied nonfiction subjects.

IN EACH UNIT

For each frame, you'll find:

An indication of what genre of writing the frames will be used for

Ready-to-reproduce booklets/reports

Pre-writing background information for the teacher to share with the students, including discussion starters and hints for possible resources

A place for the title and author of each booklet

TEACHER PAGE

Autobiography Frame

Procedure

① Discuss the term autobiography with students. Encourage children to brainstorm "ME." Allow students to share brainstorming for further idea generation.

② Gather resources. Have children create a list of questions to bring home since they may not remember events from when they were younger. Point out that this information is considered a resource.

③ **Title:** Students can title their work at any time on the line provided.

④ **By:** Students should write their name on this line.

⑤ **Picture:** Students can place a photograph (with parents' permission) or draw a picture of themselves in this box.

⑥ **Introduction:** Explain to children that an interesting opening will encourage people to read the paper. The open door icon is a way of getting people to "walk through" the door and enter into the world of the report. The opening should be interesting and informative.

⑦ **When I Was a Baby:** Information may include place of birth, birth weight, and size. Children may wish to add first words, favorite toys or stories, or a special baby memory. In the illustration box, children may want to paste a baby photo (with parents' permission). Have the children write a caption on the lines below the box. The bottle icon is a visual reminder of baby days.

⑧ **School Days:** Some children may have memories from the previous year or two. Other children may have pre-school memories. It is always helpful to brainstorm together as a class to help children recall their past experiences. It may help spark a memory! The paper and pencil icon is a visual reminder of school.

⑨ **Family:** Have children identify family members. What makes them special? Encourage children to provide details. By doing so, the audience will learn more. Note the illustration/photo box at the bottom of the page. The icon of heart and house is meant to recall family.

⑩ **Friends:** Many children enjoy writing about friends. Discuss possibilities. Friends may include peers, relatives, or pets. There are two illustration/photo boxes with caption lines. The icon of friends holding hands is used here.

⑪ **Hobbies and Interests:** Children enjoy many after-school activities that they often may not share with classmates and teachers. This section is a perfect place to share personal talents, interests, hobbies, and favorite activities. The assortment of hobbies is used as an icon.

⑫ **Closing:** Here the children can restate their purpose for writing and include something of interest and a related general statement. The conclusion should be concise. The closed door icon represents the end.

⑬ **A Timeline of My Life:** Children can use this frame to choose four key events in their life. They will record the date and event on the lines at the left. Then they can illustrate the event in the provided box. If you would like to have the students include more key events, provide multiple copies of this page to each child.

⑭ **Appendix considerations for the Autobiography Frame:**
- cover page
- table of contents
- dedication page
- labeled diagram and caption
- fascinating facts
- sequence circle
- t chart
- glossary
- bibliography

⑬

Appendix* considerations for the teacher to use to differentiate each report

Step-by-step suggestions/ guidance for all sections of the writing frame booklets, from the introduction to the conclusion

Icons to help students make connections to the different sections of the paper

Plenty of room for related illustrations

Writing prompts in each section to help guide students

Autobiography Report

Title _____

By _____

Introduction Get your reader's attention with something interesting.

Instant Nonfiction Writing Frames • Scholastic Teaching Resources

*Appendix: Additional pages to insert into the reports to differentiate and better reach the varied needs of the students

Meeting the Standards

These writing frames will help you meet these essential primary-grade writing standards:

☀ Prewriting: Uses prewriting strategies to plan written work

☀ Drafting and Revising: Uses strategies to draft and publish written work

☀ Editing and Publishing: Uses strategies to edit and publish written work

☀ Writes for different purposes (e.g., to entertain, inform, communicate, etc.)

☀ Gathers and uses information for research purposes

Source: *Mid-continent Regional Education Laboratory* (McREL), an organization that collects and synthesizes national and state K–12 standards.

Writing Frames

Animal Writing Frame

Procedure

1. Have students choose an animal of interest or assign an animal to each student or group of students.

2. Gather resources. Include books, magazines, and websites.

3. **Title:** Students can title their work at any time on the line provided.

4. **By:** Students should write their name or the names of the group members on this line.

5. **Picture:** Students can cut out or draw a picture of the animal they will be writing about.

6. **Introduction:** Explain to children that an interesting opening will encourage people to read the report. The open door icon is a way of getting people to "walk through" the door and enter into the world of the report. The opening should be interesting and informative.

7. **Appearance:** Have children describe the physical characteristics of the animal. The mirror icon will help children remember to think about a description of the animal.

8. **Behavior/Characteristics:** Encourage children to think about special qualities the animal possesses. These may include adaptations such as a polar bear's white fur or a giraffe's long neck, or behaviors such as hibernation or migration. It may also include ways of movement, communication, how they treat their young, or the animal's social interactions. The icon with three circles plus a triangle shows similar shapes and one that is different to remind students to think about some common and unique characteristics.

9. **Habitat:** Children will need to learn this important vocabulary word. Hold a discussion of various habitats. Have children identify the habitat and describe it. The house icon will help them understand the meaning of the word.

10. **Diet:** Children can identify the animal's diet. Consider introducing vocabulary words such as *carnivore*, *herbivore*, and *omnivore*. The table-setting icon is a reminder to think about food.

11. **More Interesting Facts:** This section allows children to include something special that didn't fit into any of the set topics presented. Remind them to stay focused and not to include too many additional points. The megaphone icon represents the sharing of information.

12. **Closing:** Here the children can restate their purpose for writing and include something of interest and a related general statement. The conclusion should be concise. The closed door icon represents the end.

13. **Appendix considerations for the Animal Writing Frame:**

    - cover page (first page of the Appendix)
    - about the author
    - dedication page
    - table of contents
    - labeled diagram and caption
    - Venn diagram
    - fascinating facts
    - T chart
    - glossary
    - bibliography

Title _____

By _____

Introduction Get your reader's attention.

_____

_____

_____

_____

Appearance What does this animal look like?

_____

_____

_____

_____

_____

_____

Behavior How does this animal act?

Characteristics How is it different from other animals?

_____

_____

_____

_____

_____

_____

Habitat Where does this animal live?

Diet What does this animal eat?

More Interesting Facts Tell more!

_____

_____

_____

_____

_____

_____

_____

_____

Closing Conclude and finish.

_____

_____

_____

_____

_____

_____

Autobiography Frame

Procedure

1. Discuss the term *autobiography* with students. Encourage them to brainstorm "ME." Allow students to share brainstorming for further idea generation.

2. Gather resources. Have children create a list of questions to bring home since they may not remember events from when they were younger. Point out that this information is considered a resource.

3. **Title:** Students can title their work at any time on the line provided.

4. **By:** Students should write their own name on this line.

5. **Picture:** Students can place a photograph (with parents' permission) or draw a picture of themselves in this box.

6. **Introduction:** Explain to children that an interesting opening will encourage people to read the report. The open door icon is a way of getting people to "walk through" the door and enter into the world of the report. The opening should be interesting and informative.

7. **When I Was a Baby:** Information may include place of birth, birth weight, and size. Children may wish to add first words, favorite toys or stories, or a special baby memory. In the illustration box, they may want to paste a baby photo (with parents' permission). Have the children write a caption on the lines below the box. The bottle icon is a visual reminder of baby days.

8. **School Days:** Some children may have memories from the previous year or two. Other children may have pre-school memories. It is always helpful to brainstorm together as a class to help children recall their past experiences. It may help spark a memory! The paper and pencil icon is a visual reminder of school.

9. **Family:** Have children identify family members. What makes each one special? Encourage them to provide details. By doing so, the audience will learn more. Note the illustration/photo box at the bottom of the page. The icon of heart and house is meant to recall family.

10. **Friends:** Many children enjoy writing about friends. Discuss possibilities. Friends may include peers, relatives, or pets. There are two illustration/photo boxes with caption lines. The icon of friends holding hands is used here.

11. **Hobbies and Interests:** Children enjoy many after-school activities that they often may not share with classmates and teachers. This section is a perfect place to share personal talents, interests, hobbies, and favorite activities. The assortment of hobbies is used as an icon.

12. **Closing:** Here the children can restate their purpose for writing and include something of interest and a related general statement. The conclusion should be concise. The closed door icon represents the end.

13. **A Timeline of My Life:** Children can use this frame to choose four key events in their life. They will record the date and event on the lines at the left. Then they can illustrate the event in the box provided. If you would like students to include more key events, provide multiple copies of this page to each child.

14. **Appendix considerations for the Autobiography Frame:**
    - cover page (first page of the Appendix)
    - table of contents
    - dedication page
    - labeled diagram and caption
    - fascinating facts
    - sequence circle
    - T chart
    - glossary
    - bibliography

Title _____

By _____

Introduction Get your reader's attention.

_____

_____

_____

_____

When I Was a Baby What did you do as a baby?

_____

_____

_____

_____

_____

_____

_____

_____

School Days What special school memories do you have?

_____

_____

_____

_____

_____

_____

Family Who are the people in your family? What makes them special?

_____

_____

_____

_____

_____

_____

Friends Who are the special people you spend time with?

_____

_____

_____

_____

_____

_____

_____

Hobbies and Interests What do you like to do?

_____

_____

_____

_____

_____

_____

_____

Closing Conclude and finish.

_____

_____

_____

_____

_____

_____

_____

A Timeline of My Life

Date _____

Event _____

_____

_____

_____

Date _____

Event _____

_____

_____

_____

Date _____

Event _____

_____

_____

_____

Date _____

Event _____

_____

_____

_____

Biography Frame

The biography frames can be used to write about a familiar person or a famous individual.

- Use the primary source Interview Questions Sheet (on pages 28–29) to gather information about a familiar person (parent, teacher, friend).
- Use secondary resources, such as: books, magazines, student newspapers, and websites to gather information about a famous individual.

Children can then use the biography frames provided here to help structure their reports, or they can use the interview questions to write their own reports.

Procedure

1. Discuss the term *biography* with students. Encourage children to brainstorm some famous people they would like to learn more about.

2. Gather resources such as books, magazine articles, student newspapers, and websites.

3. **Title:** Students can title their work at any time on the line provided.

4. **By:** Students should write their name on this line.

5. **Picture:** Students can place a photograph (with parents' permission) or draw a picture of the person they are writing about.

6. **Introduction:** Explain to children that an interesting opening will encourage people to read the report. The open door icon is a way of getting people to "walk through" the door and enter into the world of the report. The opening should be interesting and informative. It may begin with a question, an interesting fact, or a piece of trivia.

7. **Family Life:** Details may include place and date of birth. Information about this person's young life may include family and lifestyle. The icon of a photo album and photos will bring family life to mind.

8. **Early Life:** Children can note differences in time periods. Sometimes events or interests during childhood impact adult life. In this section, children can write about significant events of the subject's youth. The icon of a child with the word *childhood* is used to recall that period of life.

9. **Life Highlights:** Whether famous or not, everyone has some life highlights. Special events may include becoming president, discovering the light bulb, or delivering a speech. For others, a life highlight may be getting a new job, moving, winning a baseball game, or getting a part in the school play. The illustration box below includes lines for a caption. The blue ribbon icon is a reminder of something special.

10. **Challenges:** Challenges may include any life obstacle. The icon of boxing gloves represents a challenge to overcome.

11. **Other Interesting Facts:** Learning about a person includes many wonderful facts and details. This section provides a space to include more details about interesting events. The illustration box and caption lines on the following page can be used as a place to illustrate something from this section. The star icon is used to represent additional information.

12. **Closing:** Here children can restate their purpose for writing and include something of interest and a related general statement. The conclusion should be concise. The closed door icon represents the end.

13. **Important Dates:** This chart is a concise visual of dates and events. Children can write and/or illustrate in this section.

14. **Appendix considerations for the Biography Frame:**

    - cover page (first page of the Appendix)
    - table of contents
    - about the author
    - dedication page
    - fascinating facts
    - three-column chart
    - glossary
    - bibliography
    - labeled diagram and caption
    - two-box chart (change over time)

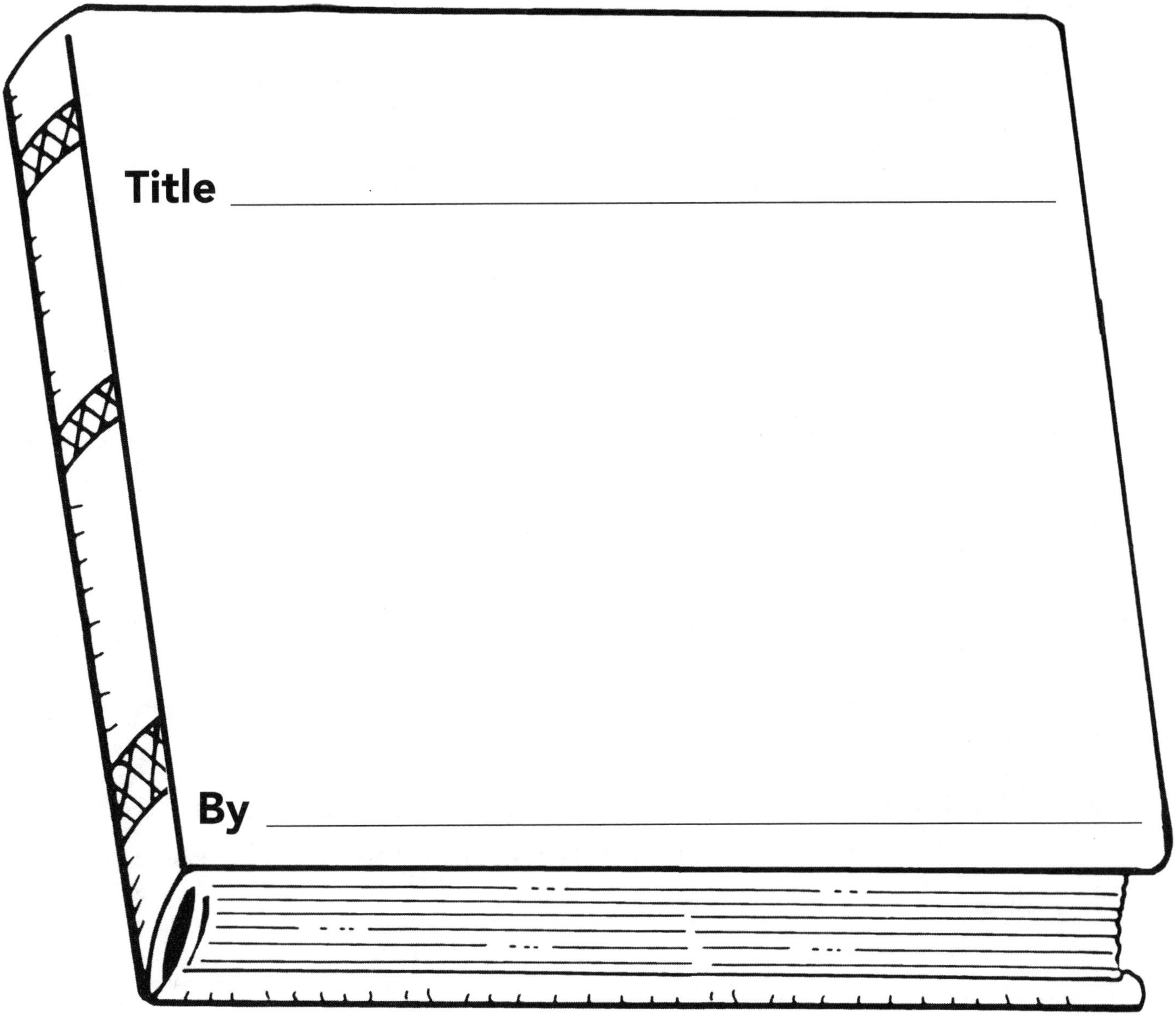

Title _____

By _____

Introduction Get your reader's attention.

_____

_____

_____

_____

Family Life Where was this person born? Describe his or her family life.

_____

_____

_____

_____

_____

_____

_____

Early Life What was life like when this person was young? Describe special interests or talents. Were there hardships or successes?

_____

_____

_____

_____

_____

_____

Life Highlights

What are some special events in this person's life?

_____

_____

_____

_____

_____

_____

_____

_____

_____

Challenges What obstacles or problems did this person encounter? How did he or she respond to challenges?

_____

_____

_____

_____

_____

_____

Other Interesting Facts What additional information did you learn about this person?

_____

_____

_____

_____

_____

_____

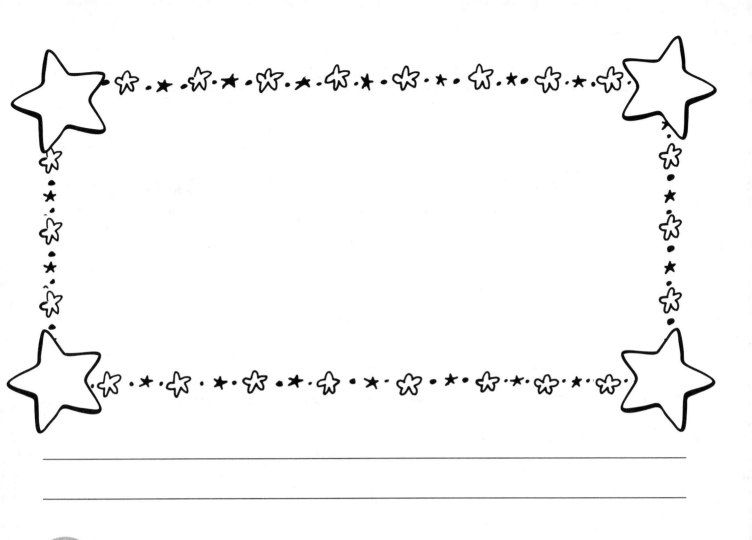

_____

_____

Closing Conclude and finish.

_____

_____

_____

_____

_____

_____

_____

Important Dates in the Life of

Dates	Important Events

Primary Source Interview Questions

In this section, primary source interview questions are provided.

Procedure

Two sets of questions are provided—one set for an adult and one set for a child. An additional blank question page is also provided.

1 Discuss what a primary source is and how to use an interview to gather information. It would be helpful to model gathering information and performing an interview. Brainstorm questions together and review how to take notes using key words. Also discuss the importance of spelling names and places correctly and recording information accurately. It is fine to ask for confirmation or to have an interviewee repeat a response for clarification.

2 The "Other Questions" page is provided so that students can create questions more specific to their needs. Discuss preparation and model how to develop appropriate questions. Remind students if they ask a question that requires only a yes or no answer, they will not get much information. Instead have the children work on questioning techniques that will result in interesting responses.

3 **Appendix considerations for the Primary Source Interview Questions:**

- cover page (first page of the Appendix)
- table of contents
- about the author
- dedication page
- labeled diagram and caption
- fascinating facts
- bibliography

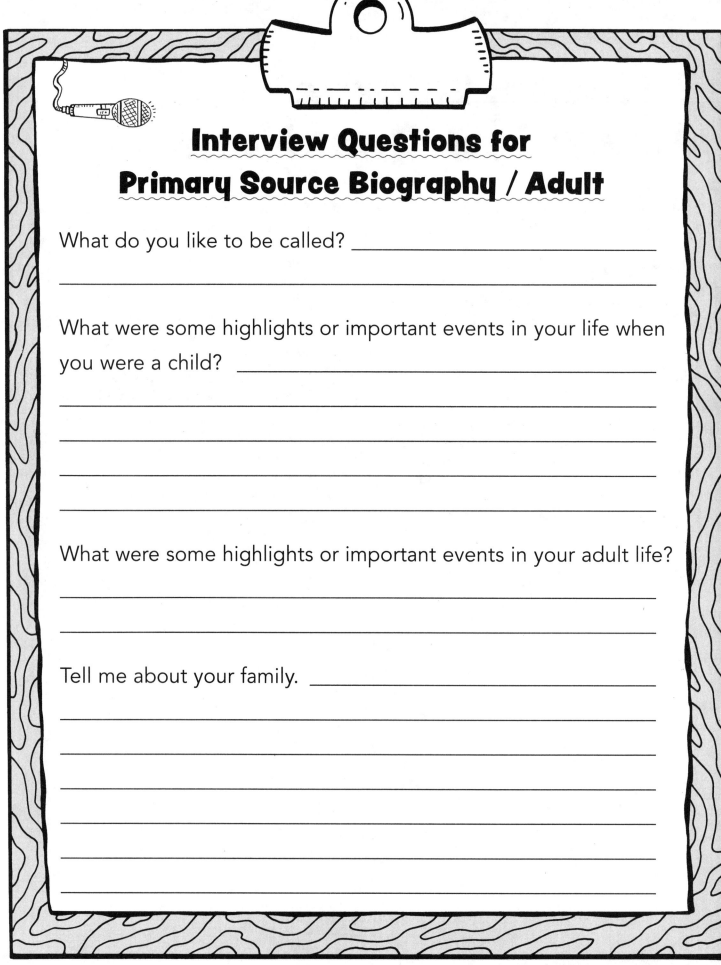

Interview Questions for
Primary Source Biography / Adult

What do you like to be called? _____

_____

What were some highlights or important events in your life when
you were a child? _____

_____

_____

_____

_____

What were some highlights or important events in your adult life?

_____

_____

Tell me about your family. _____

_____

_____

_____

_____

_____

_____

What special interests do you have? _____

_____

_____

_____

_____

What is something special about you? _____

_____

_____

_____

_____

What is your occupation (job), and what are your responsibilities?

_____

_____

_____

_____

_____

What do you like about your job, and why is it important?

_____

_____

_____

_____

_____

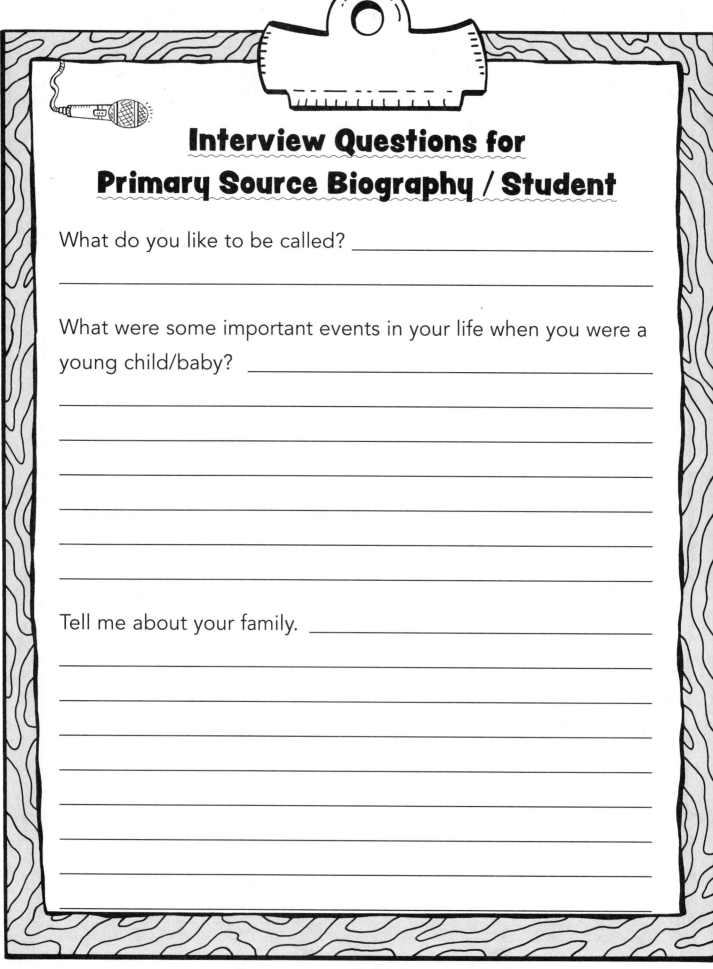

Interview Questions for
Primary Source Biography / Student

What do you like to be called? _____

_____

What were some important events in your life when you were a
young child/baby? _____

_____

_____

_____

_____

_____

_____

Tell me about your family. _____

_____

_____

_____

_____

_____

_____

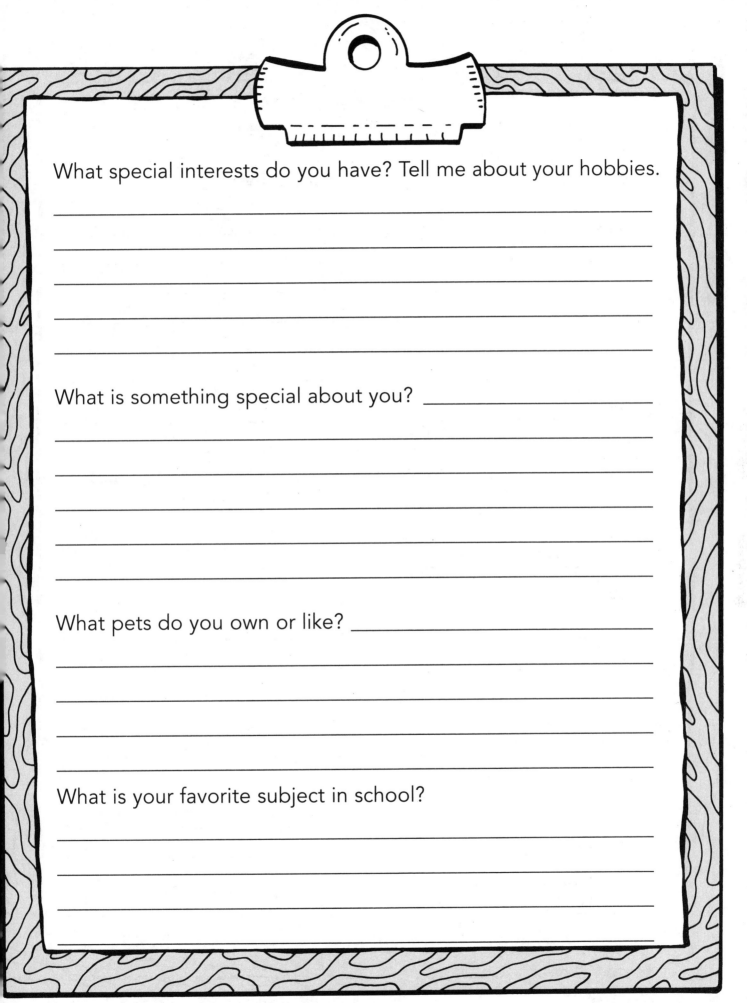

What special interests do you have? Tell me about your hobbies.

_____

_____

_____

_____

_____

What is something special about you? _____

_____

_____

_____

_____

_____

What pets do you own or like? _____

_____

_____

_____

_____

What is your favorite subject in school?

_____

_____

_____

_____

Other Questions

Interviewer:_____ **Interviewee:**_____

Question: _____
_____

Answer: _____
_____
_____
_____

Question: _____
_____

Answer: _____
_____
_____
_____

Question: _____
_____

Answer: _____
_____
_____
_____

Question: _____
_____

Answer: _____
_____
_____

"How to" Frame

Procedure

1. Have children choose a topic so that they can explain how something is done. Modeling this verbally can be fun, with one student providing directions and the other trying to follow them. Students will soon see that details are critical if they want to be accurate.

2. Discuss key words such as *first*, *then*, *next*, *after that*, and *finally*. These sequence words are important to help guide the reader.

3. **Title:** Students can title their work at any time on the line provided.

4. **By:** Students should write their name on this line.

5. **Picture:** Students can place a photograph (with parent's permission) or draw a picture of what they will be writing about.

6. **Introduction:** Explain to children that an interesting opening will encourage people to read the paper. The open door icon is a way of getting people to "walk through" the door and enter into the world of the report. The opening should be interesting and informative. It may include a reason why someone may wish to do what is being described.

7. **Number sequence:** Each step includes a key word and a number. Each step also includes a corresponding illustration/photo box and caption. Each step has its own page.

8. **Closing:** Here the children can restate their purpose for writing and include something of interest and a related general statement. The conclusion should be concise. The closed door icon represents the end.

9. **Summary:** This page can be used as a prewriting/planning page or a summary/review page. Children can use illustrations to help guide them. The key words are presented on this page to help children see the flow of the "how to" report.

10. **Appendix considerations for the "How to" Frame:**
    - cover page (first page of the Appendix)
    - table of contents
    - about the author
    - dedication page
    - fascinating facts
    - glossary
    - bibliography

Title _____

By _____

Introduction Get your reader's attention.

_____

_____

_____

First What is the first step?

_____

_____

_____

_____

_____

_____

_____

_____

Instant Nonfiction Writing Frames © 2011 by Rhonda Graff, Scholastic Teaching Resources

Then What is the second step?

_____

_____

_____

_____

_____

_____

_____

_____

Instant Nonfiction Writing Frames © 2011 by Rhonda Graff, Scholastic Teaching Resources

Next What is the third step?

_____

_____

_____

_____

_____

_____

_____

3

_____

_____

After that What is the fourth step?

_____

_____

_____

_____

_____

_____

_____

④

_____

_____

Finally What is the last step?

_____

_____

_____

_____

_____

⑤

_____

Closing Conclude and finish.

Summary

How to _____

Step	Illustration
First	
Then	
Next	
After that	
Finally	

Current Event Frame

Procedure

1 Discuss why it is important to be aware of current events. Then brainstorm places we can find current events. Children should be aware of newspapers, magazines, radio, TV, and the Internet.

2 Gather resources. Bring in a local newspaper. Use student newspapers, children's magazines, or the Internet. Discuss topics of interest and share some articles. Be sure children can identify *who, what, where, when,* and *why.* Point out that they can underline or highlight key points. Children can verbally share or create a list of these key points. Be sure to discuss validity, especially when using the Internet.

3 **Date and Source:** Model for students how to identify the date of publication and the source of the article. Record this information on the lines.

4 **Picture:** Have children cut out or draw a picture of what they will be writing about.

5 **Introduction:** Explain to children that an interesting opening will encourage people to read the report. The open door icon is a way of getting people to "walk through" the door and enter into the world of the report. The opening should be interesting and informative.

6 **Who?:** Identify the "who." The article may actually be about more than one person. The person icon represents the "who."

7 **What and Where?:** This section identifies what the article is about and where the event takes place. The icon is a light bulb, representing "what" and a globe representing "where."

8 **When?:** Have children identify when this event takes place. If a specific time is not given, they can note the publication date of the newspaper or the article. The watch icon is used to identify time. There is an illustration box and caption lines that can be used as the children wish.

9 **Why?:** This section allows the children to provide details as to why something happened. Be sure they stick to the facts. This is not a place for their opinions. The question mark icon makes them think about why something is happening.

10 **More Interesting Facts:** Although the focus is the five W's, this section provides a place to include some pertinent details. The clipboard icon is used to help students recognize other important information.

11 **Closing:** Here the children can restate their purpose for writing and include something of interest and a related general statement. The conclusion should be concise. The closed door icon represents the end. The illustration box and caption lines give them a chance to choose a highlight.

12 **Summary Chart:** This additional page provides space to gather key points and to summarize. By writing a summary statement or two, children differentiate between main idea and details. A summary should not be lengthy, but rather concise.

13 **Appendix considerations for the Current Event Frame:**

- cover page (first page of the Appendix)
- table of contents
- about the author
- dedication page
- labeled diagram and caption
- fascinating facts
- two-box chart (cause and effect)
- glossary
- bibliography

Date _____

Source _____

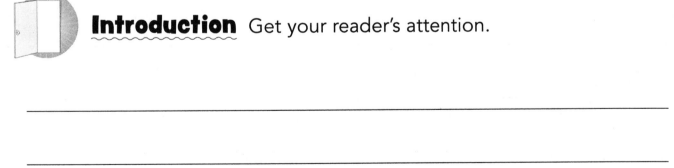

Introduction Get your reader's attention.

_____

_____

_____

_____

Who Who is involved?

What and Where What happened, and where did it happen?

When When did this take place?

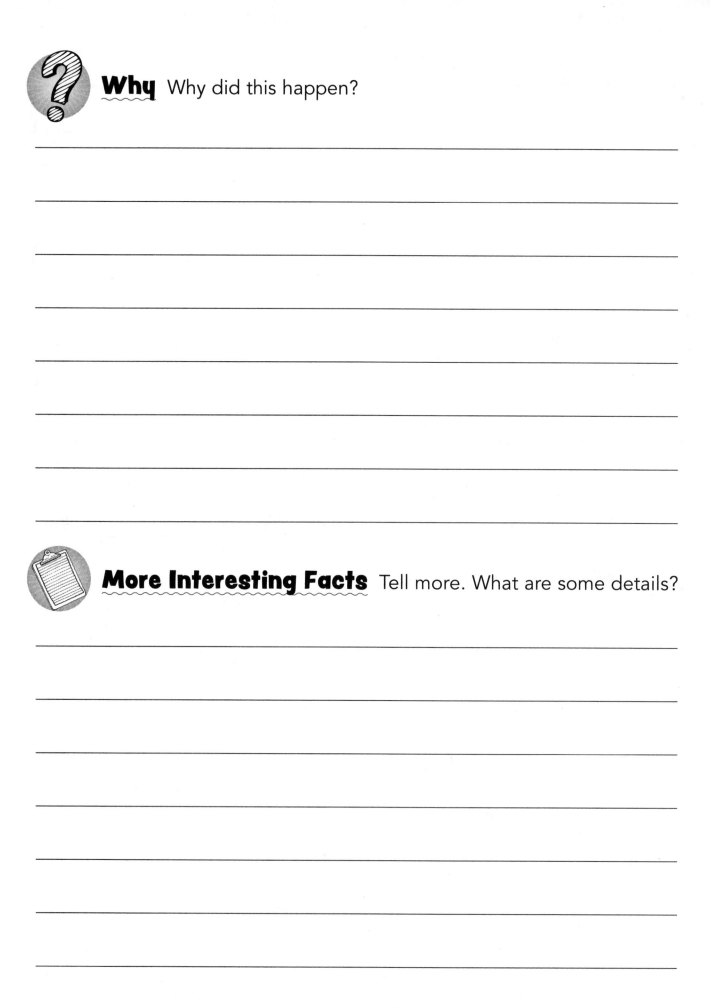

Why Why did this happen?

More Interesting Facts Tell more. What are some details?

Closing Conclude and finish.

Summary Chart

Event: _____

_____

Who?	
What?	
When?	
Where?	
Why?	

In summary, _____

_____

_____

_____

Appendix

Title _____

_____

By _____

Labeled Diagram

Caption

_____

_____

_____

Fascinating Facts

Fact 1: _____

_____

_____

_____

Fact 2: _____

_____

_____

_____

Fact 3: _____

_____

_____

_____

Fact 4: _____

_____

_____

_____

Glossary

Word: _____

Meaning: _____

_____

_____

_____

Word: _____

Meaning: _____

_____

_____

_____

Word: _____

Meaning: _____

_____

_____

_____

Bibliography

Source 1 / Book or Website: _____

_____

_____

_____

Source 2 / Book or Website: _____

_____

_____

_____

Source 3 / Book or Website: _____

_____

_____

_____

Source 4 / Book or Website: _____

_____

_____

_____

Source 5 / Book or Website: _____

_____

_____

_____

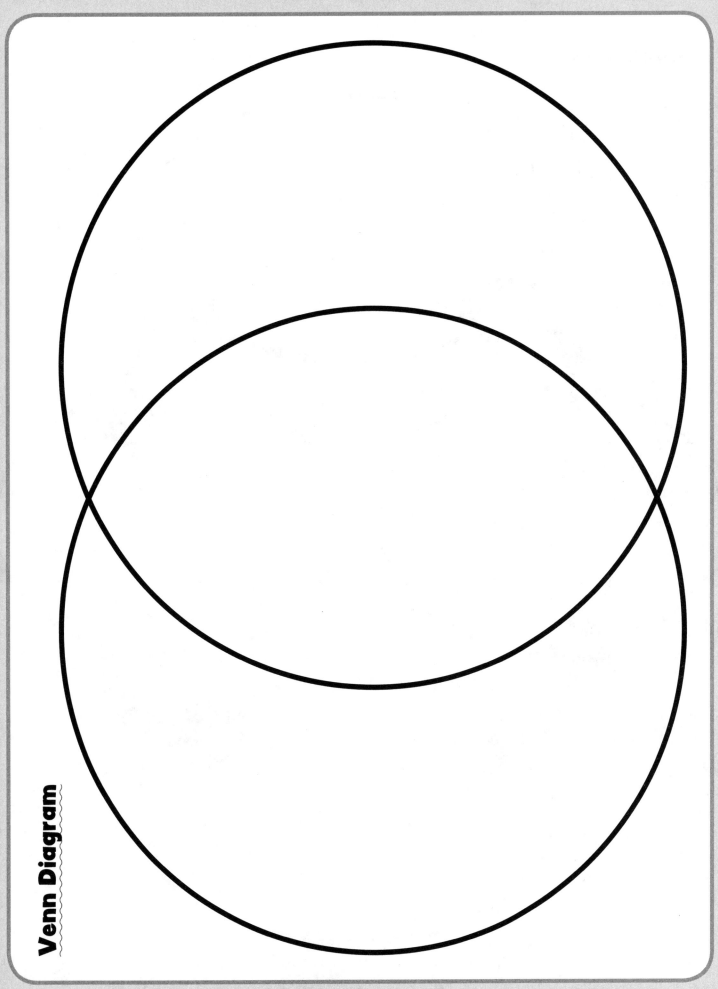

Venn Diagram

Sequence

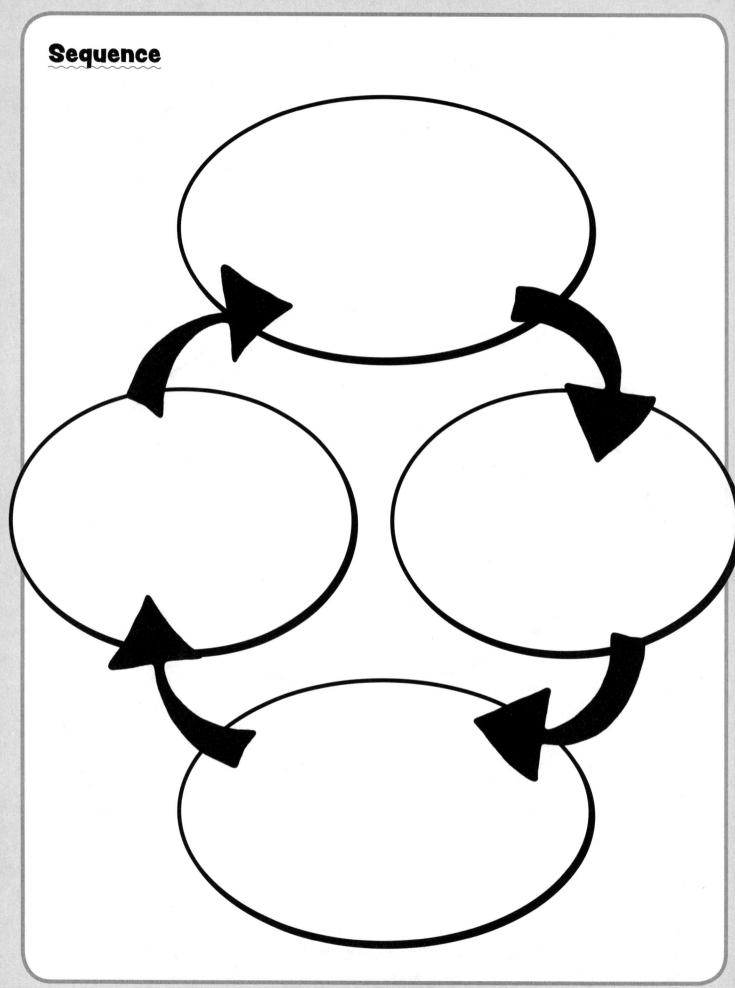

About the Author

T Chart

_____

_____

This book is dedicated to:

_____

_____

_____

© _____

Table of Contents

_____ . . . . _____

_____ . . . . _____

_____ . . . . _____

_____ . . . . _____

_____ . . . . _____

_____ . . . . _____

_____ . . . . _____

_____ . . . . _____

_____ . . . . _____

Three-Column Chart

_____

_____

Two-Box Chart

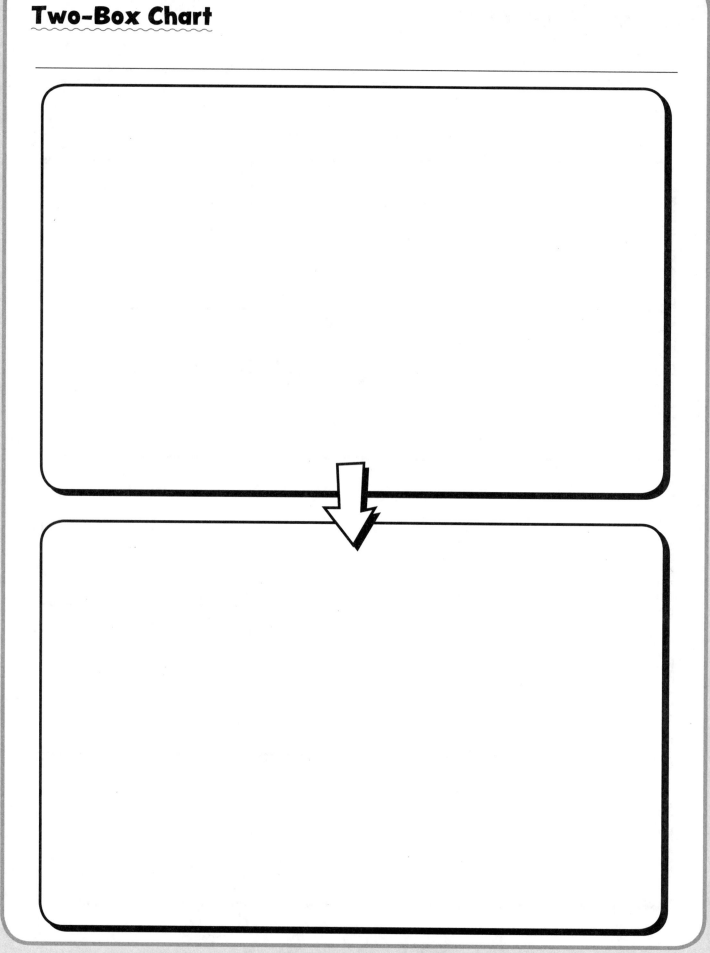

Notes

About the Author

Rhonda Graff teaches second grade at Woodglen Elementary School in New York State. She has been teaching for 20 years, covering first, second, and fifth grades. In addition, she taught a reading methods course at a local university. Rhonda enjoys being with her sons, Craig and Daniel. She also enjoys challenging herself with all forms of physical activity!